W9-ATJ-110

The Great Depression

R. Conrad Stein

$100 WILL BUY THIS CAR MUST HAVE CASH LOST ALL ON THE STOCK MARKET

CHILDREN'S PRESS
A Division of Grolier Publishing
Sherman Turnpike
Danbury, Connecticut 06816

Library of Congress Cataloging-in-Publication Data

Stein, R. Conrad.
  The great depression / by R. Conrad Stein.
    p. cm. — (Cornerstones of freedom)
  Summary: Describes the 1929 stock market crash and
the events and effects of the depression that followed,
including the New Deal programs intended to restore
the economy.
  ISBN 0-516-06668-4
  1. Depressions—1929—United States—Juvenile
literature. 2. United States—History—1933-1945—
Juvenile literature. [1. Depressions—1929.
2. United States—History—1933-1945.]
I. Title. II. Series.
E806.S7828 1993
973.91'6—dc20   93-752
[B]   CIP
                                                              AC

"**O**nce I built a railroad, made it run, made it race against time. Once I built a railroad, now it's done. Brother, can you spare a dime?" Those lines from a popular 1930s song could have been the theme of unemployed workers in 1932—the cruelest year of the Great Depression.

During an economic depression, factories dismiss laborers, stores close, and small businesses and farms fall into ruin. Short periods of depression followed by periods of prosperity have often occurred in the United States and other industrialized nations. The Great Depression of the 1930s, however, was a ten-

Unemployment Agency, *a 1937 painting by Isaac Soyer*

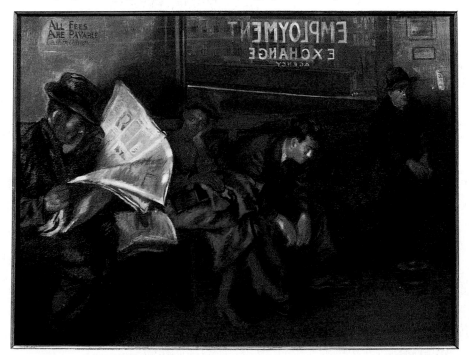

year-long economic nightmare that ended only with the onset of World War II.

Certainly not all Americans were impoverished during the 1930s. Many were unaffected by the business slump, and a few even profited from it. But for most Americans, the Great Depression struck with the impact of a flood or an earthquake. People dated their lives around it. Children would say, "We used to have ice cream for dessert, but that was before the depression." Farmers would tell each other, "I haven't been into town since the start of the depression."

The Great Depression stunned middle-class Americans, a group that had thrived in the 1920s. During that prosperous decade, families bought

During the 1920s, America prospered as never before.

In the 1930s, thousands of Americans who had never before been out of work suddenly found themselves desperately looking for ways to make ends meet.

houses, furniture, and automobiles. Then came the hard times. One young girl who lived in a comfortable house in Cleveland remembered: "All of a sudden we had to move. My father lost his job and we moved into a double garage. . . . It was awfully cold when you opened those garage doors. We would sleep with rugs over the top of us. Dress under them."

By 1932, one of every four American workers was unemployed. People who kept their jobs took deep cuts in pay. Clerks in department stores earned only five dollars a week and considered themselves lucky to be working at all. The millions of jobless people suffered indignities

Unemployed men living in a vacant lot in New York City in 1932

they never dreamed they would endure in America. Writer Edmund Wilson claimed, "There is not a garbage dump in Chicago which is not diligently haunted by the hungry. Last summer in the hot weather when the smell was sickening and the flies were thick, there were a hundred people a day coming to one of the dumps, falling on the heap of refuse as soon as the truck had pulled out and digging in it with sticks and hands."

How and when did this devastating depression begin? Economists still argue about the precise reasons for the economic collapse, but they usually trace its roots to the New York Stock Exchange and the year 1929.

At stock exchanges such as the huge one in New York City, private individuals, banks, and businesses are allowed to buy and sell shares of corporations. Owning a share is like owning a little part of a corporation. Late in the 1920s, the prices of those shares soared. In 1928, a common share of Du Pont stock increased in one year from $310 to $525. Stock in Montgomery Ward zoomed from $117 to $440. But because so many investors eagerly threw their money into the stock exchanges, the shares became overvalued. Corporate stocks simply were not worth their price tags. In September 1929, investors grew uneasy and began selling their shares in increasing numbers. This caused prices to tumble. Then came a day known in history as Black Thursday.

Happy days: the soaring New York Stock Exchange in 1929

On that day, October 24, 1929, people sold their stocks more furiously than ever before. *The New York Times* reported, "Fear struck the big investors and the little ones. . . . Thousands of them threw their holdings into the whirling stock exchange pit for whatever they would bring." In one day, investors saw the profits of several years vanish. The White Sewing Machine Company had reached forty-eight dollars a share. By the end of Black Thursday, a broker offered the stock for a dollar a share, and there were no takers. Allied Chemical stock plummeted thirty-five dollars. American Telephone and Telegraph

A stunned crowd spilled out onto Wall Street on Black Thursday, October 24, 1929. The following Tuesday, the market hit bottom when falling prices sent panicky stockholders on a selling spree.

(AT&T) fell twenty-eight dollars. But things grew even worse. On October 29–remembered as Black Tuesday–so many shares were sold that the market collapsed completely.

The stock market disaster was a blow from which the business community could not recover. Economists cite other causes for the Great Depression—a weak banking system, the fact that farmers and industrial workers had not shared in the prosperity of the 1920s, and a government that allowed businesses to do whatever they wished. But certainly Black Thursday was the beginning of the massive economic crisis that scarred the lives of millions.

The stock market crash immediately affected poor people and the middle classes, who kept their savings in banks. Many banks had invested their depositors' funds in the stock market. When the bottom fell out of the market, the banks had nothing to give their clients. Some 1,350 banks went broke in 1930 and 2,300 more failed in 1931. Millions of workers lost the savings they had scraped together over a lifetime.

Worried depositors congregate outside a failed bank in 1931.

With frightening speed, the Great Depression grew worse. Factory owners who lost money in the stock market or through bank failures could not pay their workers and were forced to dismiss them. The laid-off workers had no money with which to shop in stores, so store owners ordered fewer goods and had to lay off clerks. Because fewer goods were being ordered, the manufacturers of those goods had to lay off their workers—and so the cycle continued on and on. This downward spiral of unemployment causing more unemployment was reflected in the grim jobless figures. In 1925, only 3 percent of the nation's workers were unemployed. In 1930, that

A struggling Oklahoma farm family in 1939

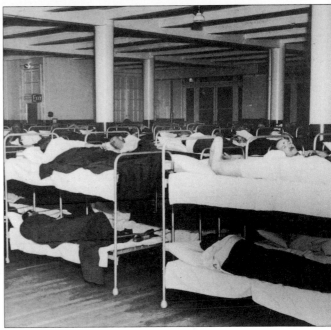

Left: A city dweller trying to make ends meet by selling sandwiches
Right: The filled bunks of a city shelter for the unemployed

figure jumped to 9 percent, and by late 1932, 25 percent of the work force was unemployed. Some 13 million people were faced with the terrifying problem of how to feed their families with no paychecks coming in.

The human suffering brought on by the depression was appalling. Families who could not pay their rent or make their mortgage payments were thrown out of their homes. Farms seized by banks for non-payment of loans were auctioned off to the highest bidder. During winter months, people spread newspapers under their clothes to ward off the cold. Others walked about with cardboard stuffed into their shoes to cover up holes. Lunch for some families consisted of bread smeared with lard. The very symbol of the

Breadlines became a common sight during the Great Depression.

depression was the breadline—a block-long line of people waiting to receive free food from a mission or welfare agency.

Years after the Great Depression ended, author Studs Terkel wrote a book called *Hard Times*. He interviewed hundreds of people who survived the depression era, and recorded their stories of how they had coped. "I can remember one time, the only thing in the house to eat was mustard," said one woman. "My sister and I put so much mustard on biscuits that we got sick. And we can't stand mustard till today." A man remembered his boyhood in the Chicago slums:

"I think it was only a nickel [for a loaf of bread]. I had to take that nickel and make sure I got it to the Maxwell Street store. . . . Coming back with that bread was full of danger, too. There was always somebody waitin' to grab it off ya. . . . I was such a good runner, later I got to be a track man." A black man from Arkansas whose parents owned a restaurant said, "I knew the depression had really hit when the lights went out. My parents could no longer pay the one-dollar [a month] electric bill."

Many Americans hoped their government would do something to ease their sufferings. Early in the depression, the country was led by President Herbert Hoover, a Republican who had been elected in 1928.

Destitute men wait in line at a soup kitchen in 1934.

Herbert Hoover

President Hoover was an intelligent, honest, and caring man. The plight of the people alarmed him, but he was a firm believer in the theory that government should not interfere with the business community. Historian Samuel Eliot Morison said of Hoover, "He was restrained from taking any bold, imaginative steps by wrong estimates of the situation, and by his philosophy, which taught him that nature would cure all whilst government intervention might ruin all."

While Hoover clung to his nonintervention philosophy, the breadlines grew longer. Angry Americans blamed their president for the crisis. Clusters of shacks set up by the homeless came

A "Hooverville" in Seattle, Washington, in 1934

Farmers were hit especially hard in the 1930s. This Montana farmer despairs over his scorched wheat fields, stripped bare by years of drought and ravenous grasshoppers.

to be called "Hoovervilles." The newspapers that the poor covered themselves with at night were nicknamed "Hoover blankets." The wild jackrabbits that people in the West were forced to eat were known as "Hoover hogs."

Complicating the industrial slump was a disaster that developed on the land. For decades, farmers on the Great Plains had plowed up natural grasses in order to plant wheat. The wheat was unable to hold the topsoil down. To make things worse, a terrible drought that lasted seven years struck the Midwest in 1931. Winds blew the dry topsoil into swirling clouds of dust so thick that they turned noon into midnight. Stripped of topsoil, thousands of once-thriving farms became barren deserts. A 50-million-acre area stretching from Texas to North Dakota became known as the Dust Bowl.

This 1935 painting by John Steuart Curry depicts yet another enemy of farmers: tornados. Dust storms and twisters destroyed many Dust Bowl farms.

In Texas and Oklahoma, farm families were forced to flee the Dust Bowl. Grimly, they packed their belongings into ancient automobiles and drove west, where they hoped to find jobs as migrant workers in the fruit and vegetable fields of California. Their sad trek was described in John Steinbeck's powerful novel *The Grapes of Wrath*: "And the migrants streamed in on the highways and their hunger was in their eyes, and their need was in their eyes. They had no argument, no system, nothing but their numbers and their needs. When there was work for a man, ten men fought for it—fought with a low wage. 'If that fella'll work for thirty cents, I'll work for twenty-five.' 'If he'll take twenty-five, I'll do it for twenty.' 'Not me, I'm hungry . . . I'll work for food.' "

John Steinbeck

During the darkest hours of the depression, farmers and workers grew so desperate that some observers believed the country was ripe for violent revolution. Then, from the state of New York, came a man whom many historians would later hail as a savior of American capitalism.

Franklin Delano Roosevelt was elected president in 1932. Even though the United States was mired in the most fearful depression of its history, his inaugural address rang like a trumpet call: "First of all, let me assert my firm belief that the only thing we have to fear is fear itself." These were bold words for the leader of a nation that seemed to be on the brink of calamity. But President Roosevelt was a bold man.

Born into a wealthy family, Roosevelt grew up in a rambling, thirty-room mansion. He entered politics as a young man and soon became a rising star in the Democratic party. Then tragedy struck the future president. While swimming, Franklin Roosevelt felt a peculiar cramp in his leg. "My left leg lagged," he later wrote. "Presently it refused to work, and then the other." Roosevelt had been stricken with polio. He would never again walk without the aid of crutches. He was only thirty-nine, but because he was disabled, many of his friends urged him to retire from

Franklin Delano Roosevelt

politics. Roosevelt refused to quit. He became the governor of New York, and was later elected the thirty-second president of the United States.

The very day he took office, in March 1933, Roosevelt faced a bank crisis. Panicky account holders rushed to their banks because they feared a massive bank failure. Roosevelt stopped the rush on the banks by declaring a "bank holiday" and closing them. He then asked Congress to pass an emergency act that would require government inspectors to examine each bank's records before allowing it to reopen.

In striking contrast to Hoover, Roosevelt marshaled the forces of government to break the grip of the depression. He launched a program called the New Deal that created dozens of government agencies and set into motion projects designed to stimulate the economy and

Posters promoting Roosevelt's New Deal

A Civilian Conservation Corps crew planting trees in Oregon

provide jobs. Many New Deal laws were passed during Roosevelt's first 100 days in office. They were the most dramatic first 100 days of any president since Abraham Lincoln.

One popular New Deal program was the Civilian Conservation Corps (CCC). It took needy young men off the city streets and put them to work in forests and national parks. There they carved out roads and hiking trails (many of which are still in use today), cleaned up beaches, and cleared camping areas. Above all, the young

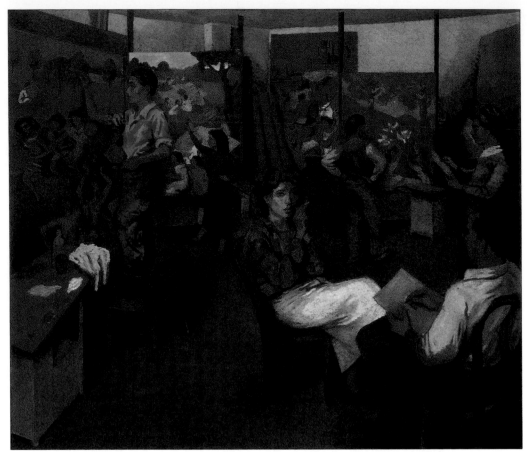

A 1935 painting by Moses Soyer depicting WPA artists at work

men planted trees. They helped to plant some 200 million trees in a hundred-mile-wide belt that stretched from Texas to the Dakotas. As the trees grew, they kept the topsoil in place, and the Dust Bowl conditions gradually ended. CCC members planted trees in every region of the country. Many of today's sprawling woodlands are the result of the CCC reforestation program.

The Works Progress Administration (WPA) provided jobs for some 2 million workers. People were put to work on projects such as slum clearance, flood control, rural electrification, and the construction of school and hospital buildings.

This allowed workers to keep their dignity by performing useful services rather than accepting welfare grants. In addition to manual workers, the WPA gave jobs to artists and writers. Artists painted murals on public buildings, and writers conducted research projects. A federal theater was formed, and hundreds of actors were hired to tour rural areas where professional theater companies had never before ventured.

The Tennessee Valley Authority (TVA) launched an ambitious construction project designed to harness the Tennessee River and provide electrical power to much of the rural South. The project was inspired largely by the vision of a remarkable senator from Nebraska named George Norris. From its start, the TVA had

The WPA hired artists to design posters promoting everything from the National Park Service (above) to WPA art exhibits (far left), to local landmarks (left).

powerful enemies. Private utility companies called the scheme socialistic. But Norris, with Roosevelt's backing, pushed the TVA law through Congress. When completed, the series of dams and power plants gave new life to what was once one of the most depressed areas in the nation.

Franklin Roosevelt also tried to bring hope to Americans through the power of his personality. There were no home television sets in the 1930s, but most families had radios. Roosevelt regularly addressed the public in a series of radio talks called fireside chats. In an informal manner, the president explained what progress his administration was making to fight the depression. Mr. Roosevelt had a warm and friendly voice. He was the first president to take full advantage of radio's ability to reach Americans in their homes.

Roosevelt was the first president to fully take advantage of radio's ability to reach the general public.

Eleanor Roosevelt visiting a school in Poughkeepsie, New York

The president's wife, Eleanor, was the most active first lady the country had ever known. A tireless worker, she visited hospitals and schools being built by New Deal funds. She had special sympathy for the nation's blacks, most of whom suffered severely because of the depression. She worked to make sure the benefits of the New Deal were shared by America's black citizens.

By the end of his first term, Roosevelt enjoyed tremendous popularity, especially among farmers and workers. More people had jobs, the banking system was sound, and large-scale government construction projects were in full swing. The 1936 election was a landslide victory for President Roosevelt. He won majorities in forty-six of the forty-eight states. His wildly happy followers sang the Roosevelt theme song, the words of which implied that the depression was over:

Happy days are here again.
The skies above are clear again.
Let us sing a song of cheer again.
Happy days are here again!

But the stubborn depression dragged on. Although millions of people worked on public projects, the recovery of the private sector was disappointing. By 1937, the jobless figures, which had begun to recede, once more approached the 10-million mark.

As the depression lingered, workers in private industry demanded pay raises and job security.

In 1938, when Louis Guglielmi painted this scene of urban hopelessness, the depression continued to linger on.

During a sit-down strike in St. Louis in 1937, auto workers passed the time by dancing.

Employers resisted their demands, and a wave of strikes swept the land.

A new technique employed by workers was the sit-down strike. Instead of walking off their jobs, factory hands simply sat in front of their machines, refused to work, and refused to leave the building. "If the boss won't talk, don't take a walk—sit down, sit down," went a popular chant. At a huge General Motors facility, sit-down strikes shut down one factory complex for six weeks. Sympathetic workers brought the strikers food and coffee. Singing and dancing troupes entertained them. When police tried to storm the buildings, the strikers pelted them with nuts, bolts, and coffee mugs.

The 1937 Republic Steel strike erupted into a violent clash between strikers and police.

Many strikes were marked by bloodshed. On Memorial Day, 1937, several thousand workers and their families paraded before the gates of the Republic Steel Plant in South Chicago. Guarding the gates were heavily armed Chicago policemen.

Angry words flew between police and strikers. Someone threw a pop bottle. Then a nightmare began. Pistols cracked. Tear-gas grenades popped. Police attacked strikers with nightsticks and pistol butts. The gunfire became a roar. Finally, ten strikers lay dead or dying, and ninety others were seriously wounded. Journalists later called the incident the Memorial Day Massacre.

Year after year of depression conditions led some Americans to listen to flamboyant leaders who claimed that only their ideas and their plans would deliver the nation from its economic turmoil. The most powerful of these self-proclaimed messiahs were Huey Long, Dr. Francis Townsend, and Father Charles Coughlin.

Huey Long built a mighty political empire as governor of Louisiana. He then became a United States senator, and had ambitions to run for president. Promising to put "a chicken in every pot," Long announced a plan that would tax rich people and provide a $5,000 house and a $2,000-per-year income for all Americans. Millions of poor people hailed him as a savior. Then, at the

Huey P. Long, Father Charles E. Coughlin, and Dr. Francis Townsend

height of his popularity, Long was gunned down by an assassin who believed he had been dishonored by the Louisiana political machine. Masses of impoverished southerners mourned Long's death.

Another advocate of sharing the wealth was Dr. Francis Townsend. His scheme for ending the depression called for giving all people over the age of sixty a pension of $200 a month. Financing this "Townsend Plan" would cost the nation more than half the money it collected in taxes. Critics pointed out that it would lead to national bankruptcy. Still, Townsend claimed to have 10 million followers, both young and old.

The most popular of the depression-era prophets was a Catholic priest from Detroit named Father Charles E. Coughlin. Known as the radio priest, Father Coughlin reached millions of homes with his weekly radio broadcasts. Father Coughlin had no grand plan to get the nation's economy rolling again. Rather, he blamed the crisis on "international bankers." Week by week his broadcasts grew more anti-Jewish, and full of praise for Hitler's Germany and Mussolini's Italy.

Even during the frustrating years of the depression, however, people found ways to have fun. Family entertainment had to be inexpensive. Chess, checkers, and card games enjoyed great popularity. A new board game—Monopoly— became an overnight rage. Americans who

During the depression, listening to the radio was as popular a family activity as watching television is today.

wondered how they would pay their rent at the end of the month delighted in using play money to buy and sell real estate and other properties.

All families enjoyed listening to radio programs. The favorites among the depression-weary people were comedy and musical-variety shows. Listeners roared at the antics of a pair of characters named Amos 'n' Andy. "Major Bowes' Amateur Hour" was a popular weekly musical show during which listeners were urged to phone in their votes for the amateur singer or musician they most enjoyed. People loved hearing crooner Rudy Vallee sing "My Time is your Time," or Kate Smith sing her theme song, "When the Moon Comes Over the Mountain." Both had regular weekly programs and enormous numbers of fans.

Kate Smith

29

Depression-era films such as Gone with the Wind *(above) and* The Wizard of Oz *(right) helped Americans escape from their troubles for a little while.*

For a special treat, a family could go to the movies. Ticket prices ranged from ten cents to twenty-five cents. Some films offered social commentary and stark depression realism. But the most successful Hollywood productions presented fantasy and escapism. More people saw the lavish Civil War drama *Gone with the Wind* than any other movie of its time. The movie fantasy *The Wizard of Oz* remains a favorite today. Writer John Dos Passos once called depression-era movies "a great bargain sale of five-and-ten-cent lusts and greeds."

By the late 1930s, the attention of Americans turned increasingly to the menacing moves of foreign dictators. The Great Depression was a worldwide calamity and contributed to the rise of totalitarian governments such as Hitler's Germany. After Hitler invaded Poland in 1939,

America began preparing for war. The increased production of weapons and other war materials gave steam to the economy and provided thousands of new jobs. But in a grim twist of irony, the United States simply slipped from one crisis into another. The 1940s brought America out of the depression—and into the bloodiest war in world history.

Today some people romanticize the hardships of the 1930s. They claim that the depression toughened Americans and was, in the long run, good for the country. But most of those who lived through the era, and felt its heartbreak, disagree. As one man told author Studs Terkel, "No, I don't see the depression as an ennobling experience. Survivors are still riding with the ghost—the ghost of those days when things came hard."

Dust-bowl refugees heading toward California in 1937

INDEX

PHOTO CREDITS

Cover, The Bettmann Archive; 1, 2, UPI/Bettmann; 3, Isaac Soyer. Employment Agency. 1937. oil on canvas, 34 ¼ x 45 in. Collection of Whitney Museum of American Art, New York. Purchase 37.44. Photography by Geoffrey Clements, NY; 4, The Bettmann Archive; 5, 6, AP/Wide World; 7, 8 (left), UPI/Bettmann; 8 (right), Stock Montage; 9, 10, The Bettmann Archive; 11, AP/Wide World; 12, UPI/Bettmann; 13, AP/Wide World; 14 (top) U.S. Bureau of Printing and Engraving; 14 (bottom), The Bettmann Archive; 15, AP/Wide World; 16, Hackley Picture Fund, Muskegon Museum of Art, Muskegon, Michigan; 17, 18 (top), UPI/Bettmann; 18 (bottom), Library of Congress; 19, UPI/Bettmann; 20, National Museum of American Art, Washington, D.C./Art Resource, NY; 21, Library of Congress; 22, 23, UPI/Bettmann; 24, National Museum of American Art, Washington, D.C./Art Resource, NY; 25, 26, 27 (right), AP/Wide World; 27 (left, middle), 29 (top), UPI/Bettmann; 29 (bottom), AP/Wide World; 30, © 1939 Turner Entertainment Co., All Rights Reserved; 31, The Bettmann Archive

Picture Identifications:
Cover: A Dust Bowl refugee family on its way west in 1936
Page 1: A New Yorker trying to sell his expensive roadster after losing all his money in the stock market crash
Page 2: Unemployed men waiting to get into a city shelter in 1930

Project Editor: Shari Joffe
Designer: Karen Yops
Photo Research: Jan Izzo
Cornerstones of Freedom Logo: David Cunningham

ABOUT THE AUTHOR

R. Conrad Stein was born and grew up in Chicago. After serving in the U.S. Marine Corps, he attended the University of Illinois, where he earned a B.A. in history. He later studied in Mexico, where he received an advanced degree in fine arts.

Reading history is Mr. Stein's hobby. He tries to bring the excitement of history to his work. He has published many history books aimed at young readers. Mr. Stein lives in Chicago with his wife and their daughter, Janna.